TRASHING THE BIBLE

CAN AMERICA SURVIVE WITHOUT THE FOUNDATION OF GOD'S WORD?

PERRY HAUPT

Copyright © 2021 by Perry Haupt.

ISBN 978-1-955885-71-3 (softcover)
ISBN 978-1-955885-72-0 (ebook)

All rights reserved. No part of this book may be reproduced or transmitted in any form or by any means, electronic or mechanical, including photocopying, recording, or by any information storage and retrieval system without express written permission from the author, except in the case of brief quotations embodied in critical reviews and certain other noncommercial uses permitted by copyright law.

Scripture quotations marked NIV are taken from the Holy Bible, New International Version®. NIV®. Copyright © 1973, 1978, 1984 by International Bible Society. Used by permission of Zondervan. All rights reserved. [Biblica]

Printed in the United States of America.

Book Vine Press
2516 Highland Dr.
Palatine, IL 60067

SUBJECTS OF INTEREST

Trashing the Bible 5

Why is God Losing the Respect that He Once Had? 8

Churches and Changing Times 13

Our Changing System of Values in the Modern World 18

Is There a Pattern for How We Should Live? 20

Is This What God Expects From Us? 22

Can We Expect Any Kind of a Turn Around? 24

Disillusioned 28

Failing Churches 31

Where Have We Gone Wrong? 35

How Can God Continue to Bless America? 40

Prayer 42

Bible Studies and Christian Book Studies 45

Church Membership 47

Feeding the Mind 49

Walking Away from God 51

Trashing the Bible: Finding God's Will for our Life, our Family, our Church 55

Mirroring God's Image as Believers, Everything we Do Must Mirror God's Image 58

Living and Abiding by Christian Principles thru Discipline 60

Question: Is Our Personal Walk Christ-Like?: Living in Holiness and Doing Good to All People 62

Application of the Gifts of the Spirit 64

Application of the Fruits of the Spirit 66

Wisdom from the Spirit 69

Having the Mind of Christ 71

Talking about Jesus 74

The Bible 79

In Conclusion 80

Take My Life and Let it Be 82

Scriptures to Contemplate 83

God's Love Letter 86

The Saving of the America We Knew: Discipline, Discipline, Discipline 89

TRASHING THE BIBLE

Yes, God's Word, THE BIBLE. How could that ever happen? We see it every day somewhere. God's Word doesn't really matter any longer in this modern world.

God surely meant well in the creation of all things. His design was so intricate that it has caused all of us, at one time or another, to stop and question, admire, wonder, and marvel at how it all came together. Nothing like it has ever been designed since.

We look at the heavens and see how all the parts of the whole were designed in perfect balance and ordered so they would perform specific duties in and thru all the earth.

God was so pleased with what he had created that he wanted to create humans in his image and likeness and for the pleasure of knowing them.

Genesis 1:26 to 31 reads like this:

Then God said, "Let us make man in our image, in our likeness, and let them rule over the fish of the sea and the birds of the air, over the livestock, over all the earth, and over all the creatures that move along the ground."

God saw all that he had made, and it was very good. What a great feeling God had with his creation.

Here is where we begin to see God as a spiritual, invisible, and personal being, creating a beautiful world with a solid foundation for each one of us. He is also all-knowing, all powerful, unchangeable, holy, eternal, and the source of all truth.

It was here where he became our heavenly father who wanted the very best for us.

It was his desire that we be obedient to him just as we are to be obedient to our earthly father.

The next scripture is found in Genesis 2 where Adam and Eve, God's first created humans, were disobedient to God and thru which SIN entered the world.

Some of the first rules for worshiping God are found in the book of Leviticus. We are to worship our heavenly Father. In Chapter 11:44-45 we find the following. I am the Lord your God; consecrate yourselves and be holy, because I am holy. Do not make yourselves unclean by any creature that moves about on the ground. I am the Lord who brought you up out of Egypt to be your God; therefore be holy, because I am holy.

A further scripture that I respect very much is the 6th Chapter of Deuteronomy which explains how we are to LOVE the Lord our God. We extract what the Jews call the Shema (the Jewish confession of faith) in verses 4 and 5. Hear, O Israel: The Lord our God, the Lord is one. Love the Lord your God with all your heart and with all your soul and with all your strength.

From all of this we are to LOVE the Lord our God as creator, sustainer, guide and friend. We are to learn to know God and keeping his covenant of LOVE.

God desires our walk with him full time. A real hand-holding experience. If we are able to do this, then it is so much easier for us to stay close to him and to do his will daily in our lives.

The state of our country and the whole world today tells us that we have cast God aside.

Our foundational Christianity is being challenged and overtaken by the things of the world which our scriptures have warned us about.

We seem to lack the passion for God's Word that once was our bedrock for living.

We see many abandoning the faith for their own desires, for political expediency, or many other distractions.

What is it about holy living that seems to be so difficult for us? Might it simply be the world in which we find ourselves today?

Here is what our scriptures have to say:

Hebrews 12:14. Make every effort to live in peace with all men and to be holy; without holiness no one will see the Lord. What a strong statement to make.

I Peter I: 13-16. Therefore, prepare your minds for action; be self-controlled; set your hope fully on the grace to be given you when Jesus Christ is revealed. As obedient children, do not conform to the evil desires you had when you lived in ignorance. But just as he who called you is holy, so be holy in all you do; for it is written: "Be holy, because I am holy."

The importance of holiness is covered in both the Old Testament and the New Testament. It is that important. God has consecrated us to be holy as he is holy.

Imagine for a moment living in pure holiness in our world.

WHY IS GOD LOSING THE RESPECT THAT HE ONCE HAD?

Our ancestors, for the most part, came to America carrying God's Word. This is what they trusted in and it helped to build a great and godly nation. This was the beginning of making us a Christian nation.

Let us not be a disappointment to their faith for our future.

Many of our great universities and hospitals carry the names of Christian church affiliations.

As a nation we have been systematically turning our backs on God. No longer can we say "We are walking with God" as he asked us to do in our scriptures.

God's Word reminds us in Genesis 6:5-9, 11-13 of the conditions of the world in Noah's time.

"The Lord saw how great man's wickedness on the earth had become, and that every inclination of the thoughts of his heart was only evil all the time. The Lord was grieved that he had made man on the earth, and his heart was filled with pain. So the Lord said, "I will wipe mankind, whom I have created, from the face of the earth—men and animals, and creatures that move along the ground, and birds of the air—for I am grieved that I have made them." But Noah found favor in the eyes of the Lord. Noah was a righteous man, blameless among the people of his time, AND HE WALKED WITH GOD.

Now the earth was corrupt in God's sight and was full of violence. God saw how corrupt the earth had become, for all the people on the earth had corrupted their ways. So God said to Noah, "I am going to put an end to all people, for the earth is filled with violence because of them. I am surely going to destroy both them and the earth".

We need to be constantly reminded of how God wants his children to live, and this is a perfect reminder.

God's all-powerful nature has been shown throughout our scriptures. Here are some supporting scriptures:

Psalm 1. "Blessed is the man who does not walk in the counsel of the wicked or stand in the way of sinners or sit in the seat of mockers. But his delight is in the law of the Lord, and on his law he meditates day and night. He is like a tree planted by streams of water, which yields its fruit in season and whose leaf does not wither. Whatever he does prospers. Not so the wicked! They are like chaff that the wind blows away. Therefore the wicked will not stand in the judgment, nor sinners in the assembly of the righteous. For the Lord watches over the way of the righteous, but the way of the wicked will perish".

What does it take to become blessed? From this scripture I believe that one must delight in walking with God, obeying his word and being rooted and grounded in his love.

2 Samuel 22:31-34. In David's Song of Praise we find this: "As for God, his way is perfect; the word of the law is flawless. He is a shield for all who take refuge in him.

For who is God besides the Lord? And who is the rock except our God? It is God who arms me with strength and makes my way perfect. He makes my feet like the feet of a deer; he enables me to stand on the heights".

A rock-solid foundation he gives us.

Our ancestors had the desire to have God as first place in their daily lives. Why else would they have taken the time, trouble and efforts to have God's name placed on so many of our local and national buildings? That name was so important to them to be able to look up to and, yet today, we have to fight to keep God in all that we do.

Psalm 33: 10-22 "The Lord foils the plans of the nations; he thwarts the purposes of the peoples. But the plans of the Lord stand firm forever, the purposes of his heart through all generations. BLESSED IS THE NATION WHOSE GOD IS THE LORD, the people he chose for his inheritance. From heaven the Lord looks down and sees all mankind; from his dwelling place he watches all who live on earth—he who forms the hearts of all, who considers everything they do. No king is saved by the size of his army; no warrior escapes by his great strength. A horse is a vain hope for deliverance; despite all its great strength it cannot save. But the eyes of the Lord are on those who fear him, on those whose hope is in his unfailing love, to deliver them from death and keep them alive in famine. We wait in hope for the Lord; he is our help and our shield. In him our hearts rejoice, for we trust in his holy name. May your unfailing love rest upon us, O Lord, even as we put our hope in you".

Why is God losing the respect that he once had?

The answer my friend is NOT blowing in the wind as the song goes. It simply lies within us who have fallen away from our creator God. Just like Adam and Eve and the hundreds upon hundreds of Israelites down thru many years. Yes, even his chosen ones.

Will America continue to slide down this slippery slope until there is NO hope? Our hope now only lies in our salvation thru Jesus, his son, whom he sent for our redemption from sin and evil.

When we trash the Bible we are really trashing God who wanted each of us to obey him and not the world and its allurements.

We all need to find a way like the apostle Paul did in Romans 12: 1-2.

"I urge you, brothers, in view of God's mercy, to offer your bodies as living sacrifices, holy and pleasing to God—this is your spiritual act of worship. Do not conform any longer to the pattern of this world, but be TRANSFORMED by the RENEWING of your mind. Then you will be able to test and approve what God's will is—his good, pleasing and perfect will".

Looking at other scriptures that support this:

1 John 2:15-17 "Do not love the world or anything in the world. If anyone loves the world, the love of the Father is not in him. For everything in the world—the cravings of sinful man, the lust of his eyes and the boasting of what he has and does—comes not from the Father but from the world. The world and its desires pass away, but the man who does the will of God lives forever".

James 4:4, 7-8 "You adulterous people, don't you know that friendship with the world is hatred toward God? Submit yourselves then to God. Resist the devil and he will flee from you. Come near to God and he will come near to you. Wash your hands you sinners and purify your hearts you double- minded".

It is quite common for those of us who name the name of Christ to live by what we believe is best for us and disregarding what God has for us and how he wants to bless us.

When we say we are truly his and call ourselves "Christian", do we really emulate the person of Jesus? Do we live by his standards and fully believe on his name?

If Jesus were to visit you or your home, what would he find you doing? Would you try to quickly put away or hide what you were into? How would you entertain Jesus when he already knows everything about you? Would you be ashamed for any reason? Maybe from now on you might find yourself doing the Jesus test so that you would be comfortable knowing that you first sought his will.

I really don't think any of us would want to be TRASHING THE BIBLE; but rather, living as God intended for us to live.

This is all very personal—about us. But if we truly all lived by the Holy Scriptures, wouldn't we find more of God's love for us in the world, more churches full and active and living spirit-filled lives rather than seeing so many failing churches in America.

What about failing churches? Let's not look at church buildings as churches but as people of God who are the church.

I am sure that most of you reading this will be able to place yourself in what I've learned in my many years of service in his name.

CHURCHES AND CHANGING TIMES

Real life in our churches has changed dramatically from what most of us remember in years gone by. Those were the days when the church people were really concerned about one another, looked after each family, and became a strong church body. The pastors were the shepherds of the congregations offering leadership in teaching, preaching, visitation, and guidance. The church body was interested in studying how to become more like Jesus, packing and shipping boxes to the mission fields, and to emulate him.

Fast forward to today when our social-economic climate has changed so much. We find ourselves living a more fast-paced life with both parents working and children growing up needing much more guidance in the home life. Teachers in the public schools find themselves trying to teach so many children lacking the discipline they should have received in the home.

Churches have taken a back seat with families struggling to make ends meet and using Sundays as personal days to do the things they could not get done during the week. Children are denied the Christian education so necessary for complete family life. Those children have become adults with their own families now and more and more we find missing from any church association at all.

Church systems are trying to attract members back into the life of the church with many different plans brought into play by professional organizations. Some are somewhat successful while others are not and the church continues to suffer.

Along with this problem we find a drastic change in personalities. Many have become very intensely impersonal and want nothing to do with church, school, or community. Try to call people today and they won't answer their phones when they see who is calling and choosing to select the ones they want to call back.

All this points to our behavioral changes that further leads us away from what has become a selfish lifestyle, and working as church, school, and community together.

The Christian lifestyle has always been one of loving, caring, and helping in a most compassionate way. Churches and community really miss that.

We all really need to get closer to God and choose his way rather than our selfish ways.

Jeremiah 29:11-13, "For I know the plans I have for you," declares the Lord, "plans to prosper you and not to harm you, plans to give you hope and a future. Then you will call upon me and come and pray to me, and I will listen to you. You will seek me and find me when you seek me with all your heart."

God's plans for many of us in the Christian community have mainly come thru working and growing together in denominational churches. With the changes in society today we find those "fences" to not be held as important as they once were. People are more inclined to move about and to search for a church body that meets the needs of their families. So many varieties of worshiping congregations are available today that offer many activities and programs that are good for the entire family. Children and youth have age- related activities designed by active leaders. Adults have their own interests in study time and helping to create meaningful church services which attract those searching for what meets their needs. Creative styles of worship services do attract many searchers who have become desirous of a change from the past where they could clock to the minute the next move in the service. Like it or not, we live in a society where change is upon us almost everywhere we go and we have grown accustomed to that in daily life. Have you ever attended a church service where there was no printed order of worship to follow? The leadership of The Holy Spirit seems to be much more exciting than following a scripted program. In many places the church has become the church of the people with the body of believers reporting in with where they saw God in action during the past week or needs of various attenders being taken care of by a loving house of believers. The mission emphasis of every church needs renewed to conform to the "Great Commission" that was set before all of us as Christian believers. Mission is to be for everyone in a church and not relegated to a certain group or committee. Churches today that have become mission churches are usually full to overflowing as God continues to bless all who do his will. The church body must learn that there is so much more to any church than a few songs, some readings, the choir anthem, the offering, and a twenty minute feel-good sermon by the pastor.

The newness of the Praise and Worship style has become unique in its own way. It does not satisfy everyone but it does attract the younger set including new families.

Where it has taken over completely, some have walked away and this is NOT what the church is all about. The leadership by the Shepherd of the congregation must see to it that there is a place for everyone. Some churches have done really well in mixing everything into one main service while larger churches have been able to have separate services.

One thing becomes very clear here as we discuss change. It was not too long after Jesus left everything in the hands of his disciples that man decided that we have something very special here and need to put all of this under OUR direction.

Thus, the advent of control by mankind with rules and regulations not necessarily according to scripture.

Pastors have become overwhelmed with large and controlling distant bodies requiring certain meetings and taking them away from the needs of the flock.

Boards and Agencies have been established, Missions have become under the control of large and expensive-to-operate sending bodies, much conforming to the desires of the ways of overseeing agencies rather than local church Deacons and Elders as was established by the Apostles.

Today there are many churches and pastors who would like to be free from such control that eats at the effectiveness of the local church.

The denominational churches in particular are having very difficult times in many ways, but mostly in losing members to the more independent churches.

Where will we go from here? What is more important? Shall we hold true to scripture or allow ourselves to be conformed to the world?

Personally, I prefer rock-solid scriptural Christianity with accountability to God rather than to the ways of mankind. We can always ask the question, what does scripture have to say on this issue?

We MUST return to God's ways and follow his leading.

Those who accept God's calling will find that he will provide all that is needed for what he wants accomplished without any stipulations from man.

When we all work to do God's will, we will never see failing churches. Failing churches happen when we develop self-interest over God's plans for our lives.

TRASHING THE BIBLE IS NOT AN OPTION.

OUR CHANGING SYSTEM OF VALUES IN THE MODERN WORLD

Values. What are values? If you consult the dictionary you might find that almost every mention of that word associates itself with things of monetary worth.

What I am talking about are the things that are most important to you. The standards by which we live.

What is it that you value the most that is NOT related to monetary worth?

People talk about values more than ever today. Everyone wants to get the best value. Churches still offer the best values. Family togetherness, Bible Studies, Learning, Making life-long friends, Helping and Praying for others while others are praying for you, Going on trips, Summer Camps, etc.

These are just some of the values that will last a lifetime and the cost to you is a few hours of your time. These kind of values have been rock-solid for many years, but the landscape is changing fast.

Now we seem to be leaning more toward things of the world. Let's look at some of what the Bible tells us about this.

I JOHN 2: 15-17, "Do not love the world or anything in the world. If anyone loves the world, the love of the father is not in him. For everything in the world—the cravings of sinful man, the lust of his eyes and the boasting of what he has and does—comes not from the father but from the world. The world and its desires pass away, but the man who does the will of God lives forever."

JAMES 4:4, "You adulterous people, don't you know that friendship with the world is hatred toward God? Anyone who chooses to be a friend of the world becomes an enemy of God."

This really tells us that we need to be extra careful not to yield to some practices just because we see our friends doing it. There are always many fads that come along and they are so easy to latch on to.

If we are in a right relationship with Jesus, then we should not have to be concerned about following worldly things. One test we can always use is this: If Jesus were here with me, would I be doing this? Think of all the many things we do that Jesus would not approve of because they are worldly and not of God.

Our hand-holding with Jesus will keep us from all kind of worldly enticements.

Proverbs 3: 5-6, "Trust in the Lord with all your heart and lean not on your own understanding; in all your ways acknowledge him, and he will make your paths straight."

Choose a rich and full life with values based on time-honored teachings from God's Word.

IS THERE A PATTERN FOR HOW WE SHOULD LIVE?

Our Holy Scriptures are full of the ways we should all live. One great guide would be to have the mind of Jesus which God gave him when he came to live among us. Jesus showed us a full life of love, caring, and compassion as he walked among the people of his day. He was so very specially gifted that people could cling to every word he said as it was so meaningful to them. Could all those we meet daily see the person of Jesus living in us by the way we conduct our lives before them?

Let's look at a little scripture to give us some guidance as to how we should live.

Very early in the Bible, God gave us, his children, the choice of LIFE or DEATH in Deuteronomy 30:15-20, "See, I set before you today life and prosperity, death and destruction. For I command you today to love the Lord your God, to walk in his ways, and to keep his commands, decrees and laws; then you will live and increase, and the Lord your God will bless you in the land you are entering to possess. But if your heart turns away and you are not obedient, and if you are drawn away to bow down to other gods and worship them, I declare to you this day that you will certainly be destroyed. You will not live long in the land you are crossing the Jordan to enter and possess. This day I call heaven and earth as witnesses against you that I have set before you LIFE and DEATH, blessings and curses. Now choose life, so that you and your children may live and that you may love the Lord your God, listen to his voice, and hold fast to him. For the Lord is your life, and he will give you many years in the land he swore to give to your fathers, Abraham, Isaac and Jacob."

1 Peter 1:13-16 and 22-25 "Therefore, prepare your minds for action; discipline yourselves; set all your hope on the grace that Jesus will bring you when he is revealed. Like obedient children, do not be conformed to the desires that you formerly had in ignorance (unknowingly). Instead, as he who called you is holy, be holy yourselves in all your conduct; for it is written, "You shall be holy, for I am holy." 22-25, "Now that you have purified your souls by your obedience to the truth so that you have genuine mutual love, love one another deeply from the heart, You have been born anew, not of perishable but of imperishable seed, through the living and enduring word of God. For "All flesh is like grass and all its glory like the flower of grass. The grass withers, and the flower falls, but the word of the Lord endures forever." That word is the good news that was announced to you.

11 Timothy 2:22-24, "Flee the evil desires of youth, and pursue righteousness, faith, love and peace, along with those who call on the Lord out of a pure heart. Don't have anything to do with foolish and stupid arguments, because you know they produce quarrels. And the Lord's servant must not quarrel; instead, he must be kind to everyone, able to teach, not resentful."

IS THIS WHAT GOD EXPECTS FROM US?

Contrary to the pattern on how we should live, the media insist on delivering the following each and every morning which is the exact opposite of living.

DRUGS
MURDERS
RAPES
KNIFE STABBINGS
SCHOOL SHOOTINGS

The breakdown in social living begins with:

ABSENCE OF A SOLID CHRISTIAN FOUNDATION AND TEACHING
LACK OF DISCIPLINE IN THE HOME
BROKEN MARRIAGE VOWS AND DIVORCE
CHILDREN SEPARATED BY DIVORCE

More modern costs to society in our worldly appetites thru:
ELECTRONIC GADGETRY
UNSUPERVISED CHILDREN TEXTING AND SEXTING
DRIVING UNDER THE INFLUENCE (DUI)

The associated costs to society such as police protection, rising insurance rates, hearings, and court costs have become necessary just to try to cover the myriad of expenditures for our reckless way of living. Then there are the on-going costs of prisons which are full to over-flowing. All of this adds to the taxes we all must bear.

Considering all of these worldly actions and choices that we make, can we agree that we are really TRASHING THE BIBLE by not living according to God's Holy Word?

CAN WE EXPECT ANY KIND OF A TURN AROUND?

What must the world think of what has become of the America they once knew?

Our historical culture has always been to welcome the whole world to a new life with opportunities for better living.

As a missionary to a foreign country, I was asked by a pastor to not tell his people about what is happening in American churches. He wanted me to continue to place American churches on a pedestal of righteousness. I simply avoided that discussion completely and continued to train his people on righteous living and to carry Jesus to everyone that they meet.

Now if this one pastor in a very small country knows about the problems facing American churches, surely many around the world already know.

What must we do to correct the path we are on?

I believe that number one is to return to full scriptural Christianity and let it begin in our seminaries.

I recently had the pleasure of recommending a young candidate for the ministry to an age-old Evangelical Christian University Seminary. After months of solid instruction, he came to me in dismay that a professor was not properly dividing the word of truth as in 11 Timothy 2:15. It became quite clear to me that this professor was not living up to the standards of this solid Evangelical Christian University.

We know that God's Word never changes. This is historically true and generally accepted by theologians everywhere.

It has become quite common to see a desire in our society to make scripture fit our life style instead of accepting what God so delicately designed for us in his Holy Word.

Once we accept his Son, Jesus, into our lives, we become a new person thru a rebirth as if to be totally born once again.

Scripture also tells us that when we become this new person that much is expected of us. This is not a close-vested personal holding of a selfish nature but rather a new life that is to be shared with everyone.

There are many arguments today that try to convince us that there are many ways to get to God. Jesus completely dispels this in John 14:6 when he says, I am the way and the truth and the life. NO ONE comes to the Father except thru me.

Then in the next chapter 15 of John he continues with what is expected of every Christian. This tends to separate all who name the name of Christ as being a Christian rather than being a true Christian believer.

He states his relationship with us in the story of The Vine and the Branches.

Jesus speaking, "I am the true vine, and my Father is the gardener. He cuts off every branch in me that bears no fruit, while every branch that does bear fruit he prunes so that it will be even more fruitful. You are already clean because of the word I have spoken to you. Remain in me and I will remain in you. No branch can bear fruit by itself; it must remain in the vine. Neither can you bear fruit unless you remain in me.

I am the vine; you are the branches. If a man remains in me and I in him, he will bear much fruit; apart from me you can do nothing. If anyone does not remain in me, he is like a branch that is thrown away and withers; such branches are picked up, thrown into the fire and burned. If you remain in me and my words remain in you, ask whatever you wish, and it will be given you. This is to my Father's glory, that you bear much fruit, showing yourselves to be my disciples.

As the Father has loved me, so have I loved you. Now remain in my love. If you obey my commands, you will remain in my love, just as I have obeyed my Father's commands and remain in his love. I have told you this so that my joy may be in you and that your joy may be complete. My command is this: Love each other as I have loved you. Greater love has no one than this, that he lay down his life for his friends. You are my friends if you do what I command. I no longer call you servants, because a servant does not know his master's business. Instead, I have called you friends, for everything that I learned from my Father I have made known to you. You did not choose me, but I chose you and appointed you to go and bear fruit—fruit that will last. Then the Father will give you whatever you ask in my name. This is my command: Love each other."

This is one of the best scriptural patterns that I know of to really live a spirit-filled life and to see a major turn-around in our way of living in America.

11 Chronicles 7:14 The Lord speaking to Solomon:

"IF MY PEOPLE, WHO ARE CALLED BY MY NAME, WILL HUMBLE THEMSELVES AND PRAY AND SEEK MY FACE AND TURN FROM THEIR WICKED WAYS, THEN I WILL HEAR FROM HEAVEN AND WILL FORGIVE THEIR SIN AND WILL HEAL THEIR LAND."

DISILLUSIONED

It is so easy to become totally disillusioned in the Protestant Christian faith if we do not see people living according to God's word and church systems failing to abide by doctrine and discipline. It seems to be a more common practice now for some church systems to not be willing to put the proper emphasis on living up to the standards which they have instituted over many years.

It is very common because of this for people to be walking quietly away from the church in which they have served so well for many years. They just seem to disappear without any concern shown by the church body.

Let's look at some possible reasons:

What is the local church teaching its people? This is a very special family time together to be learning about salvation, living the Christian life, serving others and presenting the Gospel to them, praying for their pastor, leaders, and the church body, accepting God's special calling in their lives, this list could go on and on. You might say, "people don't want to hear this anymore", but then we find them going to other churches where they claim to be getting fed.

Church bodies not being able to work together. We have been developing a selfish attitude as to what is right for me and unwilling to change to become more of an inviting church. Many times we see churches operating more like a membership club than the body of Jesus, the Christ.

We aren't serious enough about how to live the Holy Scriptures. Others see thru us and become confused.

The advent of many independent churches is being seen all over the country. People dissatisfied with hierarchy lording over them. They want more freedom to be a localized church body than to have to answer to some distant, heavily organized church system that has been designed by man rather than accepting what has been designed by God.

Churches are full of people living the good life and that is fine if they are living it as born-again Christians and fulfilling the Christian life. It is so easy to call ourselves "Christian", but do people really see Jesus living in us?

Why aren't Christians standing up today for their faith? We are living in an age of "silencing the Christian" and we have no response from any segment of Christianity to speak of. Where is the outrage? Now that doesn't sound like Jesus at all, but here is God's son who was brutally murdered for each one of us and we don't have one strong Christian in the whole world to stand up and represent all of us called Christian. Shame on us.

Disillusioned? I am not alone. There are thousands of us. Other segments of population are quick to respond to all kinds of charges that might affect them, but the lowly Christian is not to be found when Jesus needs us.

Need a little reinforcement of scripture here?

ACTS 1:8, "But you will receive POWER (emphasis mine) when the Holy Spirit comes on you; and you will be my witnesses in Jerusalem, and in all Judea and Samaria, and to the ends of the earth."

Maybe it is proper for the people called "Christian" to rise up with that kind of power. If we do not, then John Wesley's statement many years ago is coming true this very day.

"I am not afraid that the people called Methodist should ever cease to exist either in Europe or America, but I am afraid, lest they should only exist as a dead sect, having the form of religion without the power. And this undoubtedly will be the case, unless they hold fast both the doctrine, spirit, and discipline with which they first set out".

This statement should apply to all in the Christian faith.

FAILING CHURCHES

The issue of failing churches has to do with many different things. There are no easy answers nor are there any quick fixes. Current times over the many years have dictated change to be necessary. While God's Word never changes, generations, landscapes, and daily living are subject to change. The church needs to be much more aware of change. We cannot be locked into firmness from the past.

It was so very good to have so many items within our churches donated by our families over all those years. We have been good stewards of God's goodness to our churches, but we must remember that we cannot cling to the past forever. The church today must learn to adjust in many different ways just to keep a good spirit within and a lively interest in doing what God would approve of to feed the flock.

Senior church members must remember how things changed for them over the years and be willing to yield long-held traditions to keep that right spirit alive.

Possibly the liturgy of the past is not meaningful to the present age. We need to seek adjustment. The music that has drawn us closer to the Lord and warmed our hearts needs to be interspersed with appropriate praise music of the day. This has worked well in many of our smaller churches while large churches have gone to separate services just to please those who hold church music very important to them. Much of it is very important since the lyrics were written many times as testimonies of the song writer's life in the Christian faith.

I do believe that we are living in an age of creativity for more open styles of worship.

It is a matter of keeping fresh ideas working among us.

Who says we must have an order of worship printed to follow? A bulletin only for announcements, but let's begin with creativity here having the leaders directing each segment of the service by voice.

When have we ever heard of the congregation being able to express their experiences for the past week? Have they been a part of or seen a God moment at any time? Where have they seen Jesus during the past week? Can't we begin to make worship more real to people?

When did the church sanctuary become designed to look more like we were there to be entertained and the stage set for the entertainers? What about seating in ovals or circles so all people were visible to each other and we could talk freely and openly and ask questions of the pastor or leader as they presented the topic of the day?

Sound a bit off the tracks? Possibly it could work in smaller churches. Much larger churches might have to design some new ways for themselves. There should be no reason for anyone to want to hide or always sit in the same seat or in the back seat.

Why is it that back seats always fill up first? This makes it look like the custodial staff never cleans the forward seats.

Get the drift here? Why must we always keep things the same? We should all come to church in expectancy of finding love, filling of the Holy Spirit, greeting each other in the name of Jesus, to learn from the scripture being taught along with upbeat music so we don't think we are in a funeral service.

Have you ever wondered why people come to church? It seems that most come out of tradition, dedication, or it is just the thing to do on Sunday.

Some really are facing problems and troubles in their lives. This is why we must greet everyone and make them feel comfortable. A little show of LOVE goes a long way. Make them feel welcome and invite them to come back.

Many are seeking a healing from various things in their lives. We never know what a real need is and why they came to us today.

What about seekers? How can we determine a seeker? There are many in our world today and they bounce from here there and everywhere looking to be loved and to have needs satisfied.

We need to LOVE them to have Jesus in their lives. If we don't then they may end up in some other form of religion or a sect. Wouldn't that be terrible if we missed the opportunity to direct someone to Jesus for a whole new and abundant life?

There is much more of an importance in church life than most Christians show.

Is your church failing? Does it just feed the aquarium or is the time being used to teach the Bible? Many will not come to Sunday School or Bible studies but they do come to church.

This is an opportune time to teach from the pulpit. Can we even begin to imagine how we can fill needs when people get to really begin to understand scripture? They can walk away from a church service filled and refreshed with a newness of life and purpose.

What are you expecting when you go to church? This is a very good time to give this some real thought. You may uncover exactly what you have been missing.

WHERE HAVE WE GONE WRONG?

According to scripture we have gone wrong in not accepting the Bible as truth and living it daily.

The only way to know and understand God's Holy Word (The Bible) is to be taught it properly by qualified and fully experienced teachers.

I do believe that the Bible should be opened and taught from by the pastor. The students are we who call ourselves the congregation and have come prepared with our own Bibles, note pads, and writing instruments to begin to make our own personal study notes for the week ahead.

Our children will only believe it when they see us living it in the home and everywhere we go. One great weakness in America is that our children are not being taught properly in the home and the evidence is carried into our public schools.

Church is not the place to begin lively discussions about sports teams and worldly issues of any kind. We need to have our hearts set to be in tune with God in order to receive what he has for us to learn.

Good preparation and planning ahead of time is the key to having ourselves ready to be on the receiving end.

Far too many churches seem to automatically bring up many non-church issues which belong elsewhere for discussion.

Weak Christians are the prime cause of failing churches.

We are not to be an "anything goes" church. We do recognize and teach absolutes.

A real train wreck is always around the corner when we allow our discussion to get off the track.

We are all taught from day one to be a follower of Jesus. Has anyone ever asked you to become a leader for Jesus? Jesus really needs leaders today. Who will step up?

Someone once said, "Churches are trying to comfort the afflicted, but really should be afflicting the comforted". Yes, there is so much comfort from scriptures, but we need to take action based on what we learn.

Bible studies and book studies are a dime a dozen and so very enjoyable, but when on earth are we going to apply what we have learned all these years? Are we pleasing God or are we pleasing self?

Being Christian is a good sound, but living it is most difficult. Oh yes, so many are very well-meaning, but don't get very serious about it.

Who is really interested in being like Jesus? MT. 28:19-20 THE GREAT COMMISSION. Jesus left his disciples and all of us with the following order:

THEREFORE GO AND MAKE DISCIPLES OF ALL NATIONS, BAPTIZING THEM IN THE NAME OF THE FATHER, AND OF THE

SON, AND OF THE HOLY SPIRIT, AND TEACHING THEM TO OBEY EVERYTHING I HAVE COMMANDED YOU. AND SURELY I AM WITH YOU ALWAYS, TO THE VERY END OF THE AGE.

Big question? What have we done for Jesus?

It is so easy for us to discuss or argue over who it is that can baptize or give communion. I say that anyone who constitutes the elders of a church can approve of any of the faithful who desire to baptize or give communion.

There is absolutely NO need for anyone to stand around on God's white harvest mission field and not baptize immediately. Not even in the dead of winter in Russia we baptize in bathtubs.

OH, I can hear the church system people screaming now. I guess they have never had the honor of baptizing on the spot to someone who has just now found Jesus. How could anyone ever think of waiting?

Same for foot washing and communion. We are Jesus' representatives and we need to come forth and represent him.

What is it that impedes our progress? Some kind of fear? Our major problem is that we have it in our heads that only special people from the denominational fences are allowed to do this. Here we go again with those man-made rules and church system controls to bind us up from doing God's will and his work.

We have so clouded our Christian horizon that there is NO room for The Holy Spirit to come among us.

I have personally had the sad experience in one of those system churches that told me that I could not be a missionary because I did not have any cross-cultural experience, did not understand racism, did not understand sexism, etc. while all the time praising me and my wife for the wonderful work we have done in the church over many years.

I approached one person in officialdom and he wrote me a nice letter that began with, "WHEN THE CHURCH SPEAKS". Isn't that sad?

I further wrote to the Bishop asking him to kindly advise me where I might have gone wrong and what I should do now. He never gave me the courtesy of an answer.

I immediately called upon the Apostle Paul for his direction and he simply explained to me how difficult it would be for him today to be a missionary. He simply told me that he would not qualify. He advised me to go to God for direction since it was he who called me to "GO" in his name.

God proved to me that I should go since he was sending me all kinds of a prayer network of support.

My cross-cultural experience was in the university of living among the people where I was sent. Understanding the issues of racism and sexism came real easy because they knew of no such thing where I was sent.

God met me at every step and provided all that I needed along with national pastors to offer me safe direction in their country.

Have you trusted Jesus lately? I like that old song, "Step into the water, wade in a little bit deeper, deeper, come join angels singing to the lamb of God".

You see when we let go and let God have his way what a wonderful blessing it becomes for all people.

Twenty years later from that first calling we have ministered to thousands, distributed Bibles, developed or assisted six churches, began summer VBS and tent camps, provided for orphanages and serious health needs, including Chernobyl families and children.

All of those churches are on their own and we are beginning again in more small villages where they now have Bibles and we are about to teach them about Jesus.

HALLELUJAH, WHAT A SAVIOR!!

Oh yes, ONE BIBLE, but many doctrines. Only God can unite us to be his and to work for his cause and not for any home office agency.

Control is NOT scriptural. FREEDOM in Jesus, The Christ, is.

HOW CAN GOD CONTINUE TO BLESS AMERICA?

We all hear that phrase so many times and in sincerity too.

With all the dumbing down of America, the silencing of the Christians, the removal or the attempt to remove Bibles from all public places, the prayers from schools and community affairs. It just goes on and on.

How can God ever be expected to really bless America as in the past?

Who is to stand up for our rights? Where are our churches? Where are these massive church systems? Quietly hiding and possibly afraid of the consequences. We are not allowing God any room to bless us.

Too busy with other so-called important matters and living for the world.

Come on America. We are bigger than all of this. We know God is there for us and patiently waiting for us to show our colors, but he is looking for his people called "Christian" to come forward.

From the great blessings over centuries, God has much more in store for us. Look at ancient times how he blessed and he will bless again, but we must seek him and find him and do some hand-holding to show him our true LOVE and devotion to him.

Here it is in the Lamentations of the prophet, Jeremiah:

Lamentations 3:17-26. "I have been deprived of peace; I have forgotten what prosperity is. So I say, "My splendor is gone and all that I had hoped from the Lord." I remember my affliction and my wandering, the bitterness and the gall. I well remember them, and my soul is downcast within me. Yet I call this to mind and therefore I have hope:

Because of the Lord's great love we are not consumed, for his compassions never fail. They are new every morning; great is your faithfulness. I say to myself, "The Lord is my portion; therefore I will wait for him." The Lord is good to those whose hope is in him, to the one who seeks him; it is good to wait quietly for the salvation of the Lord."

While we are waiting, let's talk about PRAYER. The POWER OF PRAYER.

PRAYER

When I was around age 12 to 15 we were all encouraged to break away from the regular Wednesday night prayer service to attend a gathering of all the youth of the church. This was beyond the regular Bible teaching in this special Upper Room of our church. We were taught how to pray. Later in life I have looked back to appreciate greatly that experience in learning how to pray.

It has been noticed that few people ever learn to pray later in life. The same is true with swimming, riding a bike, etc. as it seems quite intimidating to try to learn later in public.

So what is so important about this matter of prayer? It seems that it is very important in our Christian life as Jesus taught his disciples to pray very early in their meetings.

Mt 6:5-15 is what we call The Lord's Prayer and just prior to this Jesus makes a statement about something real to pray for in Mt 5:44, "Love your enemies and PRAY for those who persecute you".

Early in the Old Testament we find the word PRAY in Deuteronomy 4:7, "What other nation is so great as to have their gods near them the way the Lord our God is near to us whenever we pray to him"?

I have always enjoyed my relationship with my Amish friends and quite often we talk about our faith. One such incident was after a gunman shot and killed innocent Amish children in a school house in Eastern Pennsylvania. It was stated by one of the Amish that day that The Lord's Prayer was all they needed to heal their hurt. I had never thought of it this way but questioned him further on his statement and then he was quick to say that The Lord's Prayer was what they live by.

Go back and read Mt 6:9-15. How often we all recite The Lord's Prayer without really understanding what we are reading. This can impact us only when we take our time to really try to understand it.

This happens much too often during our church services when we are just reading words and not given the time to fully understand what we are reading.

So what I learned in those early years about prayer was that prayer is so much like writing a letter to God.

It begins with the usual greeting in a letter of Dear God. Then the body of the letter where you communicate your reasons for writing this prayer letter like giving thanks to God, your desires, your special requests, etc. There is no need for an ending using your name as God already knows who this is that is writing to Him.

Some of us have become accustomed to hearing about prayer warriors and the power of prayer. I have taken this to understand that people using these terms are really very serious about prayer needs. The power of prayer is nothing more than prayer warriors or any group of praying people joining together to bombard heaven with our prayers.

Another very serious chain of prayer has to do with the laying on of hands for healing or blessing. James talks about this in Js. 5:13-16 as the Prayer of Faith.

"Is any one of you in trouble? He should pray. Is anyone happy? Let him sing songs of praise. Is any one of you sick? He should call the elders of the church to pray over him and anoint him with oil in the name of the Lord. And the prayer offered in faith will make the sick person well; the Lord will raise him up. If he has sinned, he will be forgiven. Therefore confess your sins to each other and pray for each other so that you may be healed. The prayer of a righteous man is powerful and effective."

James apparently had some good first-hand experience with God's healing power thru prayer.

Who or what is it that you are praying for today and every day until you receive an answer?

Has prayer made a difference in your Christian walk?

BIBLE STUDIES AND CHRISTIAN BOOK STUDIES

What a marvelous way to help to learn the factual truth about the Bible AND what authors have to write about their experiences based on the Holy Scriptures.

Spending good time learning all of this places us in a very special way to impart our learning to those who have never heard the GOOD NEWS.

Unfortunately most of the time it turns out to be just for our own understanding.

This mirrors the image that most Christians get from these studies and from our hours spent in church services.

It seems as though it is all about us and not really to be shared with anyone else. Rather selfish I think.

Why keep this GOOD NEWS just for our own edification?

Most other book learning in our society we readily share with others.

Over many years I heard the expression, "They are so hungry for God's Word". When it came time for me to get some first-hand experience with this, I found it very true as in one place we distributed $7,000 worth of Bibles to over 1,000 people.

In mission work this is the catalyst that brings people together for study and for beginning a church. No trashing of the Bible here as it is used to bring the lost to Christ.

Why, then, is God's Word becoming of less importance in our culture?

John 5:39-40 Jesus said, "You diligently study the Scriptures because you think that by them you possess eternal life. These are the Scriptures that testify about me, yet you refuse to come to me to have life".

CHURCH MEMBERSHIP

Church membership is a good thing for it gives all families a sense of belonging together, growing together, and working together to help build the kingdom of God.

Young families in particular need this kind of church family for many reasons that go beyond those mentioned above.

Years of time have shown me how you can make Christian friends for life who grow thru Bible studies, children and youth work, and serving in various capacities in all types of church work.

All this good activity needs to stop short of giving members a false security that church membership alone is the gateway to heaven.

Scripture never mentions church membership per se and teaches very special steps toward salvation and the fullness of life throughout eternity.

We will always have seekers and those who seem to never quite find the real church home to attend regularly.

In today's life we find more church shopping than I can ever remember what it is that will satisfy us.

People do have real needs. They always have, but I believe that today a more complexity of concerns fill our daily lives. How can anyone find the perfect answer they are searching for?

My counsel would be to begin searching God's Word, the Bible, in conjunction with looking for a church that has a regular on-going Bible study where you can meet, learn, discuss, and begin to find the answers to all your concerns and needs. This method will undoubtedly lead you to a real desire to begin a church membership.

I am trying to paint another good reason to establish a long and lasting church membership.

FEEDING THE MIND

Just as we feed our bodies, wholesome and healthy food to keep us fit and trim, so we should be feeding our minds good, healthy reading material.

We gain good, solid information in reading and studying the Bible and books by fully committed Christian authors. Also Christian seminars, listening to Christian radio and TV programs and even listening to music by any number of Christian artists.

Today we have so much to choose from, but far too often I do believe we fill "The Temple of The Holy Spirit", our bodies, where God abides with totally unrelated material than the wholesome, uplifting material that is so very accessible in our society.

God is trying to bring us back to him which the Bible calls "The Sheepfold" or into his loving care.

Do you remember the early day of computers? "Garbage in—Garbage out" was a handy phrase which warned us that if we wanted to receive good information then we must be very careful with the entries made to our computers.

Can you imagine what our minds take in every 24 hours? Do we have a filtering system or do we just let 'er flow. The more the better so to speak.

We are children of our heavenly Father who has designed the entire universe for all the good and great things that are beneficial for us.

Our culture is so messed up today and we wonder how this ever came about.

In the next chapter we will become very specific about this trend. It is entitled, "Walking Away From God"

WALKING AWAY FROM GOD

God has lavished his grace upon us in such abundance that he even gave us his only son, Jesus, to die for our transgressions and sins so that each one of us can receive full pardon, salvation and an abundant life in him throughout all eternity.

Grace is simply God's unmerited favor upon each of us. This shows how much God really loves us, his children. He wants us to have the very best that he has to offer us.

So, what have we been doing? Accepting, receiving, opening his gift to us or have we been choosing to do anything and everything according to our own desires?

Once in Biblical history there was a specific time frame where the Israelites had no king and everyone did as he saw fit. Judges 21:24.

Yes, we are at that point in America today and around the world.

Another very fitting scripture the prophet Isaiah recorded in Isaiah 5:20, "Woe to those who call evil good and good evil". The same is happening today in America. Please continue reading all of Isaiah chapter 5, especially the "Woes and Judgments" from verse 8 to 30.

Anyone nervous now as to what is happening to America, the land that we all love?

Remember Kate Smith singing, "God Bless America"? God is doing his very best to stand beside her and guide her. Yes, God is trying and at the same time we insist on "TRASHING THE BIBLE". We have allowed ourselves to become politically correct in removing God from most everywhere while at the same time trying to "Silence the Christians".

Let's return to a time of greatness in America and to the timeline she has followed.

When our soldiers returned home from WWII they found few jobs to employ those thousands. Many left home again, this time seeking employment. They went to places like Akron, Ohio and the tire industry and to the Buffalo, NY area for work in the steel works at Lackawanna.

Family earnings began to rise as did the purchase of goods and services.

America had new life. Oh, the great feeling it was to be home, to be loved, to be productive and if any were poor, their Christian brothers and sisters were there to take care of family needs thru their churches.

NO welfare here!! In ill health or poverty the government helped some thru the county homes of those days.

Television entered the homes around 1947-48 and that began to have a major impact on the family, the church and community as competition entered the scene.

In Pennsylvania there were what they called, "Blue Laws" which closed the majority of businesses on Sunday and supported family worship until years later when they were removed.

All of a sudden we saw God being taken out of our schools and public life, Bible reading in schools, the ten commandments taken out of our government offices and more.

Now we have so much electronic gadgetry and much more that has contributed to the weakness in church families.

And so, slowly but surely over many years we have been "Walking Away From God" as if we don't need a heavenly Father any longer.

Our ways of living have changed. Our values have changed.

Our beliefs have changed. Our morals have changed. Our ways have changed. Our culture has changed.

We are SO divided on Politics, Economics, Immigration, Race and Religion.

On issues such as, Abortion, Same Sex Marriage, World Events, Drugs and Alcohol, Sexting, Cheating, Children and Internet Meetings with Strangers, Children at a Loss for Proper Parenting, and on and on it goes. Even in our Society of Faith we have Bishops Trashing the Church Discipline along with the Bible thinking that they know better than God.

Our FREEDOMS and FREE SPEECH are being challenged.

Now we must all think twice or several times before we speak or we will be cited for HATE SPEECH.

The RUDENESS of the interview process on TV talk shows. What is that teaching our youth when people constantly butt in on discussions? No respect to allow each person to finish talking. How did this develop?

What has happened to our most Blessed and Beloved America? WHY? You don't suppose so much of this today is because we have been "Walking Away From God"? I do believe this is very true and that we really are—

TRASHING THE BIBLE

Finding God's Will for our Life, our Family, our Church

It's all about TRANSFORMATION—a complete change in our life, and we acknowledge that thru BAPTISM.

Beginning the walk to discover and discern God's will.

Romans 12:1, The Apostle Paul is addressing the saved here. "Therefore, I urge you, brothers, in view of God's mercy, to offer your bodies as living sacrifices, holy and pleasing to God—this is your spiritual act of worship."

Romans 12:2, Paul is speaking about total sacrifice to God's will and way for our life.

"Do not conform any longer to the pattern of this world, but be TRANSFORMED by the RENEWING of your mind. Then you will be able to test and approve what God's will is—his good, pleasing and perfect will."

Steps in the journey beyond Romans 12:2: PRAYER—Your daily, personal time with God.

BIBLE—Getting to know the scriptures. Psalm 119:10. "Your word is a lamp to my feet and a light for my path".

Circumstances of life:

Acts 3:1-10, Peter and John were on the way to pray at the temple—not expecting to heal a man.

"One day Peter and John were going up to the temple at the time of prayer—at three in the afternoon. Now a man crippled from birth was being carried to the temple gate called Beautiful, where he was put every day to beg from those going into the temple courts. When he saw Peter and John about to enter, he asked them for money. Peter looked straight at him, as did John. Then Peter said, "Look at us!" So the man gave them his attention, expecting to get something from them.

Then Peter said, "Silver or gold I do not have, but what I have I give you. In the name of Jesus Christ of Nazareth, walk." Taking him by the right hand, he helped him up and instantly the man's feet and ankles became strong. He jumped to his feet and began to walk.

Then he went with them into the temple courts, walking and jumping, and praising God. When all the people saw him walking and praising God, they recognized him as the same man who used to sit begging at the temple gate called Beautiful, and they were filled with wonder and amazement at what had happened to him.

Wise counsel from godly, trusted people.

Exodus 33:13-14. Moses speaking. "If you are pleased with me, teach me your ways so I may know you and continue to find favor with you. Remember that this nation is your people." The Lord replied, "My Presence will go with you, and I will give you rest."

Do you listen to your pastor and other saved ones for wise counsel? Success in our journey (Romans 12:2 above).

Our DESTINATION: God's good, pleasing, and perfect will. Our DISCIPLINE: Not conforming, but transforming.

Our DEDICATION: Sacrificing all and giving up self.

The DIFFERENCE: Peace and Joy—Not unrest and sorrow.

MIRRORING GOD'S IMAGE AS BELIEVERS, EVERYTHING WE DO MUST MIRROR GOD'S IMAGE

We see God thru his son, Jesus. When God sent Jesus to us, only then did we get a more complete image of God.

So, to mirror God's image we must mirror Jesus' image.

What is that image Jesus portrayed? Love, Joy, Peace, Compassion, Caring, Wisdom, Holiness, Grace, and we could go on and on with many more like all the fruits of the Spirit listed in Galatians 5: 22-25.

How could this be possible coming from sinners such as we are? This is a very large order to fill. Possibly one step at a time, one characteristic at a time, but always moving toward holiness. WHAT A GOAL!!

We must all realize that we are human in a fallen world and God knows that. This is why he is very patient with us and any slight improvement he would count as some degree of success.

We can ponder over much of this just as we ponder over all of Jesus' teachings, but until we have that discipline to take the first step forward we will never accomplish much by standing still.

Possibly we need to become more goal-oriented on these points. We must admit that we all need help to do this so let us look at some scriptural advice.

First we must look at our Christian leaders as in I Thess. 5:13 which says, "Hold them in the highest regard in love because of their work. Live in peace with each other".

Then look for a reason to do this like in Eph. 2:10. "For we are God's workmanship, created in Christ Jesus to do good works, which God prepared in advance for us to do".

Then we must change our ways like in Romans 12:1-2.

Next, we must demonstrate action such as in Galatians 6:10. "Therefore as we have opportunity, let us do good to all people, especially to those who belong to the family of believers".

Finally, read all of Paul's letters to the various churches which gives us plenty of instructions as our platform or foundation.

Is it possible for us to mirror God's image? To emulate Jesus? This is the goal we must set for ourselves.

LIVING AND ABIDING BY CHRISTIAN PRINCIPLES THRU DISCIPLINE

In most of our lives we have learned that personal discipline is very important. If we discipline ourselves to get up early in the morning, we find that we can get much good work done before friends and others come around.

If we set our sights on what we want to accomplish in a day, we must discipline ourselves to achieve our goal. We have already learned that life goes much better for us if we have good discipline.

Now, what is it like to live our Christian lives with good discipline? Will people be able to see that we are committed Christians by the way we discipline our lives in everything we do?

In Titus 1:8-9 Paul is speaking to his friend, Titus, about elders and leaders in the church. In the entire book of Titus, Paul is giving instructions as to how Christians should behave. He instructs Titus to tell the truth (and sometimes we know that the truth hurts) and further instructs him on how to be a good Christian leader in the church. He tells us that we all need to be upright, in control of our lives, holy and disciplined before God and the world.

Many others are watching us and our Christian behavior. He also tells Titus, his young son in the faith, that he must hold firmly (disciplined) to the trustworthy message he has been taught so that many others can see Jesus living in him.

This would be a great encouragement to all who are watching us called Christians and for them to see how we do everything in accordance with his word as in II Corinthians 9:8 and Ephesians 2:10.

If we are to be seen as Christ-ones (Christians), then we need not only to know scripture but to live it so others can see Christ living in us.

QUESTION: IS OUR PERSONAL WALK CHRIST-LIKE?

Living in Holiness and Doing Good to All People

Hebrews 12:14 "Make every effort to live in peace with all men and to be holy, without holiness no one will see the Lord".

Galatians 6:10 "Therefore, as we have opportunity, let us do good to all people, especially to those who belong to the family of believers".

It is one thing for us to study the Bible, but quite another thing to apply it daily in our lives everywhere that we go.

Can we show Jesus to the world around us by what we have learned from him?

The church (his church) is not a self-serving body. We must take from our church gathering a very large message to the whole world outside of the church building.

We cannot be called a social gathering. We are a worshipping, spiritual gathering.

I know that it is difficult for us who have all been taught reality all our life to be able to learn about spirituality. Spirituality cannot be taught. Pastors and others can teach about it, but it is the Holy Spirit who reveals himself in many different ways and not necessarily the same way to each one of us.

Now, where are we as so-called Christians on this subject? Think about it, if you will. Are we living the Gospel? Are we carrying the Gospel? Are we sharing the Gospel? Are we emulating Jesus?

Consider Jesus and God's purpose he had for sending his son to us.

Would Jesus be pleased with our lives and our behavior if he came to visit us?

Where will we go from here? When we go to church on Sunday, is it just another one of those Sunday-go-to-meeting days?

Can Jesus count on us to be truly his and willing to die for his cause?

With all the troubles and problems in our world, where are the people called Christian? It seems to be easier just to turn this all over to para-church organizations rather than for us to stand up for Jesus. This is the old "Let George Do It Approach".

Luke 18:8, "When the son of man comes, will he find FAITH on the earth?"

APPLICATION OF THE GIFTS OF THE SPIRIT

One part of church life that I have found overlooked is the understanding and application of the GIFTS of the SPIRIT. These gifts are all God-given and are to be used for the edification and building up of the church. Sadly, we do not study them enough to begin to understand what they can do for a church. As you read each one below, take time to dwell on them asking the guidance of the Holy Spirit to see which one or ones have been given to you specifically—not for any selfish, personal use but for the good of the entire church.

They appear in several different scriptures:

Romans 12:6-8, "We have different gifts, according to the grace given us. If a man's gift is PROPHESYING, let him use it in proportion to his faith. If it is SERVING, let him serve; if it is TEACHING, let him teach; if it is ENCOURAGING, let him encourage; if it is CONTRIBUTING TO THE NEEDS OF OTHERS, let him give generously; if it is LEADERSHIP. let him govern diligently, if it is SHOWING MERCY, let him do it cheerfully".

1 Corinthians 12:4-11, "There are different kinds of gifts, but the same Spirit. There are different kinds of service, but the same Lord. There are different kinds of working, but the same God works all of them in all men. Now to each one the manifestation of the Spirit is given for the common good. To one there is given through the Spirit the message of WISDOM, to another the message of KNOWLEDGE by means of the same Spirit, to another FAITH by the same Spirit, to another gifts of HEALING by that one Spirit, to another MIRACULOUS POWERS, to another PROPHECY, to another DISTINGUISHING BETWEEN SPIRITS, to another speaking in different kinds of TONGUES, and to still another the INTERPRETATION OF TONGUES. All these are the work of one and the same Spirit, and he gives them to each one, just as he determines".

FOR WHAT PURPOSE WERE THESE GIFTS GIVEN?

Ephesians 4:11-12, "It was he who gave some to be apostles, some to be prophets, some to be evangelists, and some to be pastors and teachers, to prepare God's people for works of service, so that the body of Christ may be built up until we all reach unity in the faith and in the knowledge of the son of God and become mature, attaining to the whole measure of the fullness of Christ".

APPLICATION OF THE FRUITS OF THE SPIRIT

Galatians 5:22-26, "But the fruit of the Spirit is LOVE, JOY, PEACE, PATIENCE, KINDNESS, GOODNESS, FAITHFULNESS, GENTLENESS, and SELF-CONTROL.

Against such things there is no law. Those who belong to Christ Jesus have crucified the sinful nature with its passions and desires. Since we live by the Spirit, let us keep in step with the Spirit. Let us not become conceited, provoking and envying each other".

So, since we, as Christians, live by the Spirit, we need to keep in step with the Spirit.

By us living closely with God, he will always live with us and show us all the FRUITS of the Spirit plus all his goodness and everlasting life.

What application of these FRUITS do we need?

John 14:15-21, THE PROMISE OF THE HOLY SPIRIT
Matthew 5:13-16, SALT AND LIGHT
Matthew 6:24, WHOM WILL YOU SERVE?

Matthew 7:19-20, BY OUR FRUITS WE WILL BE KNOWN AS HIS.

How, then, shall we live?

God promises us real life if we choose to live in him, and his promises are true.

Many times the world gets in our way and can cause us to go astray from his word, but through his love for each one of us, his children, he accepts us and welcomes us back home. Remember the story of the Prodigal Son? No questions asked—just come on back home.

Where is he in your life today? Is he abiding or just nearby for when you need him?

Complete surrender will bring us a life filled with the FRUITS OF THE SPIRIT and all his goodness that he has promised to each one of us who fully commits our life to him.

For believers living in the love of God and by the FRUITS OF THE SPIRIT:

The love of God is greater far than any of us can imagine. It goes beyond the farthest star and reaches to the lowest hell. Now that is a far piece and it goes even beyond that.

What portion of that degree of love can we show and where and how often do we share it?

Is the love of God providing for us—even if we don't deserve it? That is called GRACE.

Are we truly believers? Do we really believe without seeing miracles? Refer to John 20:30-31. What does it take for us to become full believers?

God brings us all up out of deep troubles and he visits us with his Holy Spirit.

Many times he leaves us speechless.

Will we allow the person of the Holy Spirit to be exalted in our body? Read what Paul had to say in the book of Philippians 1:20-21.

LOVE your neighbor as yourself, Mt. 22:37-39. LOVE your enemies. Lk. 6:35-36.

You are my disciples if you LOVE one another. John 13:34-35.

All of this leads us toward a full Christian life by the FRUITS OF THE SPIRIT.

WISDOM FROM THE SPIRIT

Corinthians 2:6-16, "We do, however, speak a message of wisdom among the mature, but not the wisdom of this age or the rulers of this age, who are coming to nothing. No, we speak of God's secret wisdom, a wisdom that has been hidden and that God destined for our glory before time began. None of the rulers of this age understood it, for if they had, they would not have crucified the Lord of glory. However, as it is written: "No eye has seen, no ear has heard, no mind has conceived what God has prepared for those who love him." But God has revealed it to us by his Spirit.

The Spirit searches all things, even the deep things of God. For who among men knows the thoughts of a man except the man's spirit within him? In the same way no one knows the thoughts of God except the Spirit of God. We have not received the spirit of the world but the Spirit who is from God, that we may understand what God has freely given us. This is what we speak, not in words taught us by human wisdom but in words taught by the Spirit, expressing spiritual truths in spiritual words. THE MAN WITHOUT THE SPIRIT DOES NOT ACCEPT THE THINGS THAT COME FROM THE SPIRIT OF GOD, FOR THEY

ARE FOOLISHNESS TO HIM, AND HE CANNOT UNDERSTAND THEM BECAUSE THEY ARE

SPIRITUALLY DISCERNED. The spiritual man makes judgments about all things, but he himself is not subject to any man's judgment: "For who has known the mind of the Lord that he may instruct him?"

BUT WE HAVE THE MIND OF CHRIST.

HAVING THE MIND OF CHRIST

WE ACCEPT CHRIST AS SAVIOR.

THE HOLY SPIRIT COMES TO LIVE WITHIN US. WE GROW IN THIS LIFE UNTIL:

WE MAKE A BIG DECISION THAT WE WANT TO BE MORE LIKE JESUS.

THEN WE MUST SEARCH "THE MIND OF CHRIST" TO SEE IF WE CAN REALLY QUALIFY TO HAVE "THE MIND OF CHRIST"

THIS WILL BE ANOTHER BUILDING BLOCK IN THIS NEW LIFE FOR US. IT WILL BE A GOOD FOUNDATION FOR OUR FAITH.

THE STANDARD BY WHICH WE MUST MEASURE OUR LIVES IS TO CONSIDER THE PERFECT LIFE OF JESUS:

TO LOVE AS HE LOVED: LUKE 10:27, JOHN 13:34, LUKE 10:38-42

TO WALK AS HE WALKED: 1 JOHN 2:6, 1 PETER 2:21-24

TO BE HOLY AS HE IS HOLY: 1 PETER 1:13-16, HEBREWS 12:14, ROMANS 12:1

TO FOLLOW HIS EXAMPLE IN WORD AND DEED: JOHN 14:6, GALATIANS 2:20

TO THINK AS HE THOUGHT: 1 CORINTHIANS 2:6-16, HEBREWS 3:1

TO HAVE HIS ATTITUDE: PHILIPPIANS 2:5-11, 2 COR 10:5, ROMANS 12:2

CAN WE DO ALL OF THE ABOVE? NAME THEM AGAIN (A-F) CAN WE DO THEM PART OF THE TIME? ALL THE TIME?

CAN WE LOVE AS HE LOVED? ALL THE TIME? DO WE REALLY KNOW UNSELFISH LOVE? CAN WE SHOW LOVE TO EVEN THE WORST PEOPLE?

CAN WE REALLY FOLLOW IN HIS STEPS? HOW IS OUR HOLINESS IN ALL THAT WE DO? ARE WE HIS EXAMPLES IN WORD AND DEED? COULD WE POSSIBLY THINK AS HE DID?

WHAT ATTITUDES DO PEOPLE SEE IN US?

COULD WE POSSIBLY BE CRUCIFIED WITH CHRIST LIKE PAUL SAID SO CHRIST COULD LIVE IN US?

HOW MUCH DO WE REALLY WANT TO BE LIKE JESUS? ARE WE WILLING TO PAY THE COST?

CAN WE GIVE UP OUR SELFISH THINGS OF THE WORLD?

IF JESUS CAME TO OUR HOUSE TODAY—WOULD WE RECOGNIZE HIM? HOW WOULD WE REACT? WHAT WOULD WE DO? WHERE WOULD WE GO?

I THINK YOU MIGHT WANT TO ASK HIM MANY QUESTIONS THAT MAY NOT BE ANSWERED IN GOD'S WORD.

JESUS WOULD WANT EACH OF US TO BE VERY HONEST WITH OURSELVES.

LET'S DO A TEST PATTERN AND PRETEND THAT JESUS IS WALKING BESIDE US. WOULD IT MAKE A DIFFERENCE IN YOUR LIFE?

IS OUR DESIRE TO BE LIKE HIM?

TALKING ABOUT JESUS

I began this book by talking about God and how instrumental he is in our lives IF we allow him to be.

At this point I think it wise to consider Jesus and the fact that God sent his son to be our redeemer and savior.

We have covered much scripture but not enough priority on the life of Jesus.

His life was certainly well documented and most of us have studied that in Sunday School as well as reading books and seeing movies on his life.

Like the Bible, it is good to have knowledge about all of this but how can we take this knowledge and do something with it.

I am most certain that Jesus would like to have us much closer to him than we seem to be, but our experience tells us that he is not an everyday subject.

We see some reminders about him on vehicles like the symbol of a fish or a few bumper stickers, but not much else unless we find it in church.

How can we carry Jesus out from church? I guess it is probably very quietly as we have found that the majority of people get offended by the mention of his name.

It is much easier and more accepted to talk about worldly things than to speak about the one who holds our life in his hands and helps prepare the way for eternal life with him.

Church bulletin boards hardly ever mention his name or sermon titles, but rather cute phrases that draw our attention to make us smile or laugh.

Advertising can work miracles as we know. The Fall season always brings a lot of interest in football. On Saturday mornings we see traffic headed toward college football games with flags a-flying as fans of favorite football teams. Ever consider what impression we would make doing the same on Sunday mornings as we headed to church? WOWZERS!!! What attention that would bring. NO, we still want to enter our church buildings quietly, reverently, as if to hold Jesus silently and in very personal, high regards.

Here is the man that God chose for us to live by. He sent the angel, Gabriel, to announce to the virgin, Mary, that she would be with child and give birth to a son and that she was to give him the name of JESUS. He came rather quietly into the world as the SON OF GOD and to humble, earthly parents.

He spent his early life growing up in Nazareth where his father was a carpenter. At a very young age he astounded the teachers of his day in the temple as he showed knowledge far beyond years. Although his ministry was only short-lived, he performed much in teaching, miracles, and healings.

God's purpose in sending his only son, Jesus, was to show all of us what God the Father was like. God soon saw that his own son was not well liked by the rulers of his day. He became a threat to their very well-established life.

Jesus' chosen disciples had great difficulty in understanding his spiritual nature, and therefore had a problem interpreting much of the meaning in what he was saying because it was not real to them. They, like we, had been taught only about reality.

Finally, Jesus had to admit that he was God in the flesh, and that set off a fire-storm of hatred toward him to the point they accused him of blasphemy and put him to death.

The cross was a very heavy burden for him to bear, but he knew that he must fulfill God's plan to be crucified, buried, and resurrected to walk among them again and then to ascend to God, His Father, in heaven.

All the people were astounded as nothing like this had ever happened before. His closest followers and his very own disciples were left confused, and yet amazed, by all of this.

The resurrection and post-resurrection experiences were very difficult for them to comprehend. This became totally mind-boggling. Much of what Jesus told them earlier in their walk with him now began to jolt their minds and challenge their thoughts.

It was not finished yet, for Jesus promised his very own that when he went to heaven he would send a Comforter to take his place and live within each of us, if we accepted him as Lord and Savior of our lives.

Then along came the ascension which left them dumbfounded.

A series of events that Jesus talked openly about had now taken place and such fear gripped them that they went into hiding for fear of their lives.

After 50 days, this Comforter that Jesus talked about came to them as the promised Holy Spirit. Jesus had also told them earlier that they would receive POWER when the Holy Spirit came and that they were to be his witnesses in all the earth—everywhere. Acts 1:1-11

Many Christians today are much like the disciples. Close to Jesus, but still not believers.

The Bible is God's Word. Historically correct, well documented, and yet we fail to believe it. It took Peter quite a while to become a full believer. It is recorded in Acts Chapter 2.

Now Peter remembers all that Jesus said and can see through it. It took the personal intervention in the life of Saul with a miraculous visitation before he believed and became the Apostle Paul. Acts Chapter 9.

How long and how much proof do we need to become full believers?

We say that we love Jesus. We say that he comforts us. We sing about him. We talk about him, but do we share his message with others?

We need to prepare ourselves to receive him into our everyday lives as THE ONE whom God sent to save us and redeem us from sin and to set us apart for life eternal. ARE WE PREPARED?

Signs are everywhere around us. It will be like the description that Jesus gives in Matthew Chapter 24.

Remember—He gave the GREATEST GIFT OF ALL WHEN HE GAVE JESUS. We need to unwrap his GIFT and feel all the LOVE that God has for each of us.

What will we do with Jesus?

THE BIBLE

"This book is the mind of God, the state of man, the way of salvation, the doom of sinners, the happiness of believers. Its doctrines are holy, its precepts are binding, its histories are true, and its decisions immutable.

Read it to be wise, believe it to be safe, practice it to be holy. It contains light to direct you, food to support you, and comfort to cheer you. It is the traveler's map, the pilgrim's staff, the pilot's compass, the soldier's sword, and the Christian's character. Here paradise is restored, heaven opened, and the gates of hell disclosed. Christ is its grand subject; our good, its design; and the glory of God, its end. It should fill the memory, rule the heart, and guide the feet. Read it slowly, frequently, prayerfully. It is a mine of wealth, a paradise of glory, and a river of pleasure. Follow its precepts and it will lead you to Calvary, to the empty tomb, to a resurrected life in Christ; yes, to glory itself, for eternity." –author unknown.

IN CONCLUSION

If you have been able to finish this book, I must wonder what various thoughts it has generated in your mind.

I must admit that some of this is a bit radical when we compare it with church as we know it today.

What has our Christian walk told us?

God was radical, Jesus certainly was, the reformers were, and to this day we have those who think differently. Why would that be? All radicalism has been meant to get attention.

God had to be radical with the Israelites to get them to see thru their fallacies. Jesus had to be radical with the rulers of his day to show them in person what God was really like.

The reformers had to use radical ideas to show churches of their day that they were not always following God's intent thru scripture.

In all cases it caused confusion, disbelief, persecution, and hate.

Very few people like change. Most of us are set in our ways, but in all of history God has called us back to his sheepfold.

So, what makes us think that we need more radical thinking in the church today?

Our assignment that Jesus first gave to his disciples, which carries on thru to us as disciples today, was a very specific calling to reach out to the lost.

I really have to question that intent in most church services of today.

Interestingly enough, and in this writer's defense, let's look at what Jesus had to say:

Mt 5:11-12, Jesus said, "Blessed are you when people insult you, persecute you and falsely say all kinds of evil against you because of me.

Rejoice and be glad, because great is your reward in heaven, for in the same way they persecuted the prophets who were before you".

John 15:18-19, Jesus is also speaking, "If the world hates you, keep in mind that it hated me first. If you belonged to the world, it would love you as its own. As it is, you do not belong to the world, but I have chosen you out of the world. That is why the world hates you."

So, if there be any arousing of hate toward this writer for this publication, we all need to remember that it has all come down thru a lengthy history about what our heavenly father has intended for each of us as to how to live.

TAKE MY LIFE AND LET IT BE

Take my life and let it be, Consecrated Lord to thee;

Take my moments and my days, Let
them flow in ceaseless praise.

Take my hands and let them move, At the impulse of thy love;
Take my feet and let them be, Swift and beautiful for thee.

Take my voice and let me sing, Always, only for my King; Take
my lips and let them be, filled with messages from thee.

Take my silver and my gold, Not a mite would I with-hold; Take
my intellect and use, Every power as thou shalt choose.

Take my will and make it thine, It shall be no longer mine;
Take my heart it is thine own, It shall be thy royal throne.

Take my love my Lord I pour, At thy feet its treasure
store; Take myself and I will be, Ever, only, all for thee.

EVER, ONLY, ALL FOR THEE

—Frances Havergal

SCRIPTURES TO CONTEMPLATE

Psalm 14:1, THE FOOL SAYS IN HIS HEART, "THERE IS NO GOD."

Psalm 33:12, BLESSED IS THE NATION WHOSE GOD IS THE LORD, THE PEOPLE HE CHOSE FOR HIS INHERITANCE.

Psalm 32:8, I WILL INSTRUCT YOU AND TEACH YOU IN THE WAY YOU SHOULD GO; I WILL COUNSEL YOU AND WATCH OVER YOU.

Psalm 8, O LORD, OUR LORD, HOW MAJESTIC IS YOUR NAME IN ALL THE EARTH! YOU HAVE SET YOUR GLORY ABOVE THE HEAVENS. FROM THE LIPS OF CHILDREN AND INFANTS YOU HAVE ORDAINED PRAISE BECAUSE OF YOUR ENEMIES, TO SILENCE THE FOE AND THE AVENGER.

WHEN I CONSIDER YOUR HEAVENS, THE WORK OF YOUR FINGERS, THE MOON AND THE STARS, WHICH YOU HAVE SET IN PLACE, WHAT IS MAN THAT YOU ARE MINDFUL OF HIM, AND THE SON OF MAN THAT YOU CARE FOR HIM? YOU MADE HIM A LITTLE LOWER THAN THE HEAVENLY BEINGS AND CROWNED HIM WITH GLORY AND HONOR. YOU MADE HIM RULER OVER THE WORKS OF YOUR HANDS; YOU PUT EVERYTHING UNDER HIS FEET: ALL FLOCKS AND HERDS, AND THE BEASTS OF THE FIELDS, THE BIRDS OF THE AIR,

AND THE FISH OF THE SEA, ALL THAT SWIM THE PATHS OF THE SEAS.

O LORD OUR LORD, HOW MAJESTIC IS YOUR NAME IN ALL THE EARTH!

Isaiah 40:31, BUT THOSE WHO HOPE IN THE LORD WILL RENEW THEIR STRENGTH. THEY WILL SOAR ON WINGS LIKE EAGLES; THEY WILL RUN AND NOT GROW WEARY, THEY WILL WALK AND NOT BE FAINT.

Matthew 6:33, BUT SEEK YE FIRST THE KINGDOM OF GOD, AND HIS RIGHTEOUSNESS; AND ALL THESE THINGS SHALL BE ADDED UNTO YOU.

Proverbs 3:5-6, TRUST IN THE LORD WITH ALL YOUR HEART AND LEAN NOT ON YOUR OWN UNDERSTANDING; IN ALL YOUR WAYS ACKNOWLEDGE HIM, AND HE WILL MAKE YOUR PATHS STRAIGHT.

Isaiah 40:28-29, DO YOU NOT KNOW? HAVE YOU NOT HEARD?

THE LORD IS THE EVERLASTING GOD, THE CREATOR OF THE ENDS OF THE EARTH. HE WILL NOT GROW TIRED OR WEARY, AND HIS UNDERSTANDING NO ONE CAN FATHOM. HE GIVES STRENGTH TO THE WEARY AND INCREASES THE POWER OF THE WEAK.

Corinthians 1:3-4, PRAISE BE TO THE GOD AND FATHER OF OUR LORD JESUS CHRIST, THE FATHER OF COMPASSION AND THE GOD OF ALL COMFORT, WHO COMFORTS US IN ALL OUR TROUBLES, SO THAT WE CAN COMFORT THOSE IN ANY TROUBLE WITH THE COMFORT WE OURSELVES HAVE RECEIVED FROM GOD.

Deuteronomy 4:2, DO NOT ADD TO WHAT I COMMAND YOU AND DO NOT SUBTRACT FROM IT, BUT KEEP THE COMMANDS OF THE LORD YOUR GOD THAT I GIVE YOU.

GOD'S LOVE LETTER

My Child,

You may not know me, but I know everything about you. Psalm 139:1. I know when you sit down and when you rise up. Psalm 139:2.

I am familiar with all your ways. Psalm 139:3. Even the very hairs on your head are all numbered. Matthew 10:29-31. For you were made in my image. Genesis 1:27. In me you live and move and have your being. Acts 17:28. For you are my offspring. Acts 17:28. I knew you even before you were conceived. Jeremiah 1:4-5. I chose you when I planned creation. Ephesians 1:11-12. You were not a mistake, for all your days are written in my book. Psalm 139:15-16. I determined the exact time of your birth and where you would live. Acts 17:26. You are fearfully and wonderfully made. Psalm 139:14. I knit you together in your mother's womb. Psalm 139:13. And brought you forth on the day you were born. Psalm 71:6. I have been misrepresented by those who don't know me. John 8:41-44. I am not distant and angry, but am the complete expression of love. 1 John 4:16. And it is my desire to lavish my love on you. 1 John 3:1. Simply because you are my child and I am your father. 1 John 3:1. I offer you more than your earthly father ever could. Matthew 7:11. For I am the perfect father. Matthew 5:8. Every good gift that you receive comes from my hand. James 1:17. For I am your provider and I meet all your needs. Matthew 6:31-33. My plan for your future has always been filled with hope. Jeremiah 29:11. Because I love you with an everlasting love. Jeremiah 31:3. My thoughts toward you are countless as the sand on the seashore. Psalm 139:17-18. And I rejoice over you with singing. Zephaniah 3:17. I will never stop doing good to you. Jeremiah 32:40. For you are my treasured possession. Exodus 19:5. I desire to establish you with all my heart and all my soul. Jeremiah 32:41. And I want to show you great and marvelous things. Jeremiah 33:3. If you seek me with all your heart, you will find me. Deuteronomy 4:29. Delight in me and I will give you the desires of your heart. Psalm 37:4. For it is I who gave you those desires. Philippians 2:13. I am able to do more for you than you could possibly imagine. Ephesians 3:20. For I am your greatest encourager. 2 Thessalonians 2:16-17. I am also the father who comforts you in all your troubles. 2 Corinthians 1:3-4. When you are brokenhearted, I am close to you. Psalm 34:18. As a shepherd carries a lamb, I have carried you close to my heart. Isaiah 40:11. One day I will wipe away every tear from your eyes. Revelation 21:3-4. And I'll take away all the pain you have suffered on this earth. Revelation 21:3-4. I am your father and I love you even as I love my son, Jesus. John 17:23. For in Jesus, my love for you is revealed. John 17:26. He is the exact representation of my being. Hebrews 1:3. He came to demonstrate that I am for you, not against you. Romans 8:31. And to tell you that I am not counting your sins. 2 Corinthians 5:18-

19. Jesus died so that you and I could be reconciled. 2 Corinthians 5:18-19. His death was the ultimate expression of my love for you. 1 John 4:10. I gave up everything I loved that I might gain your love. Romans 8:31-32. If you receive the gift of my son, Jesus, you receive me. 1 John 2:23. And nothing will ever separate

you from my love again. Romans 8:38-39. Come home and I'll throw the biggest party heaven has ever seen. Luke 15:7. I have always been father and will always be father. Ephesians 3:14-15. My question is—will you be my child? John 1:12-13. I am waiting for you. Luke 15:11-32.

Love, Your Dad,
Almighty God

THE SAVING OF THE AMERICA WE KNEW

Discipline, Discipline, Discipline.

Can we believe that "The Trashing Of The Bible" can be stopped today simply by the way we live? Is it possible to begin a new day of encouraging events in America by joining hands and minds together for the restoration in our lives of God's Holy Word, The Bible?

Will this be our desire or will we be content to watch all the good that America has to offer slipping away because we have chosen to lose sight of the foundational values from the Bible that has made America great?

It is so easy to make changes and to set laws, rules, and regulations with the hope in mind that it will be for the betterment in our lives. Many times this does work, but when it does not it is very difficult to change or revert back to the way it used to be.

This could be how it might affect us as we see that we desire a more positive change for America than what we are seeing today.

I can assure you that this will be very difficult. We see how our country has changed from being one of a majority agreeing on most any issue to a very marginal acceptance or denial.

History has proved that change is very difficult. It will take extreme discipline to return to God's Word.

Could we possibly find that degree of Biblical discipline in our daily life? Where would we begin? Surely it would begin in the homes of America and this could start with teaching from the Bible. The very first result would probably be in the public school classrooms. The teachers would recognize it immediately. The parents would carry this discipline into the workplace and possibly begin to change attitudes of workers about honesty and production. Management might even be influenced to join in. Bring all this back home to the workings within our communities as to how we can serve better and develop better programs in our towns and cities. A true ripple effect for positive change and living.

Now take all of this from our communities into local government where the big decisions are made having to do with every phase of our life-styles in our local communities. Possibly we can move on forward to influence our state and federal government. Wouldn't that be a marvelous and unique way to begin a positive change in America?

It can be done. All it takes is the desire to see a better America because we have the right to affect change for the good of all Americans thru the discipline that we have learned and shared from the Bible.

NO MORE "TRASHING OF THE BIBLE" FOR NOW WE CAN SEE CLEARLY HOW WE ALL CAN BE MOTIVATED FOR GOOD AND THE SAVING OF THE AMERICA WE ONCE KNEW.

CPSIA information can be obtained
at www.ICGtesting.com
Printed in the USA
BVHW072332011022
648340BV00002B/5